TRUTH MAY BE STRANGER THAN FICTION. BUT WHICH IS *FUNNIER*?

Albert Einstein
THEORETICAL PHYSICIST

"I first realized I was blessed with above-average intelligence when my classmates began referring to me as 'Einstein.' "

Queen Isabella
MONARCH OF SPAIN

"A crueler, more gentile nation."
—announcing the Spanish Inquisition, 1492

John Kennedy, Jr.
SEXIEST PUBLISHER ALIVE

"Hi."
—surefire pickup line

Karl Marx
MARXIST

"From each according to ability. To each according to his needs. Plus tax and tip."
—splitting the bill with a bunch of friends at a restaurant

Clarence Thomas
SUPREME COURT JUSTICE

"I'll have what Scalia's having."
—decision on lunch

Francis of Assisi
SAINT

"Who are you calling Assisi?"

QUANTITY SALES

Most Dell books are available at special quantity discounts when purchased in bulk by corporations, organizations, or groups. Special imprints, messages, and excerpts can be produced to meet your needs. For more information, write to: Dell Publishing, 1540 Broadway, New York, NY 10036. Attention: Special Markets.

INDIVIDUAL SALES

Are there any Dell books you want but cannot find in your local stores? If so, you can order them directly from us. You can get any Dell book currently in print. For a complete up-to-date listing of our books and information on how to order, write to: Dell Readers Service, Box DR, 1540 Broadway, New York, NY 10036.

I AM NOT A CORPSE!

AND OTHER QUOTES NEVER ACTUALLY SAID

MARK KATZ

A DELL BOOK

A DELL TRADE PAPERBACK
Published by
Dell Publishing
a division of
Bantam Doubleday Dell Publishing Group, Inc.
1540 Broadway
New York, New York 10036

Library of Congress Cataloging in Publication Data

Katz, Mark.
    ''I am not a corpse!'' : and other quotes never actually said / Mark
    Katz.
        p.   cm.
    ISBN 0-440-50712-X
    1. Quotations.   2. Wit and humor.   I. Title.
PN6162.K36   1996
818'.5402—dc20   95-39367
                                                             CIP

Printed in the United States of America

Published simultaneously in Canada

July 1996

10   9   8   7   6   5   4   3   2   1
FFG

for money

ACKNOWLEDGMENTS

When I was writing a regular humor column for my college newspaper, a friend once suggested my byline ought to be "by Mark Katz and a cast of thousands."

Ten years later, that process of showing, sharing, and seeking opinion produced this book as well. I am indebted to dozens—an assortment of friends, relatives, friends of friends, relatives of friends of friends, and strangers I met on buses.

Many thanks to Kris Dahl at ICM, who somehow got a book deal for a person whose only literary credential was a library card. And to Leslie Schnur, Betsy Bundschuh, Kristin Kiser, and Kathleen Jayes at Dell, editors who believed in this book and made it better.

More thanks to ~~very~~ good friends and ~~extremely~~ funny people who pitched and punched-up quotes: Tracy Abbott, Cindy Chupack, Alan Mandel, Rich Rosenthal, Evan I. Schwartz, and one who also contributed a title, Erik Tarloff. Not to mention my brother Robert, who I came close to not mentioning.

And the many who gave thoughtful advice and/or generous feedback: Steven Akey, Rich Albert and Brenda Haas, Tom Allon, Mark Ansorge, Aunt Dianne, Don Baer, Bob Barnett, Tom Barreca, Paul Begala, Amy Bolotin, Christopher Buckley, Lisa Buksbaum and Boxtree Communications, Michael Caruso, Larry and Deidre

Cohen, Ellen Creager, Jonathan Fisher, Jonathan Foster, Mitchell Fox, Andrew Frank, Jeff Frankel, Mark Gearan, Michael Kanef, Andrew Katz, Jay Kriegel, Jack Leslie, Emily McKann, Brad Mazarin, Brandon Moglen, John Mooney, Dee Dee Myers, Kirk O'Donnell, Roger Poirier, Jonathan Prince, Max Reynal, Pam Abel Reynal, Rica Rodman, Ilene Rosensweig, Phil Rosenthal, Andy Savitz (who could have been a big help had he called me back), John Scanlon, Shepardson Stern & Kaminsky—and then some, Mark Shields, siblings Bruce and Ruth, Prof. Joel H. Silbey, Karen Sonet-Rosenthal, George Stephanopoulos, The Tribunal (Patti Solis, Scoop Cohen, and John Hart), Lorraine Voles, Jill Wilkins, Jeff Winikow, E. Bingo Wyer, and the Writers' Guild TIP-EAST sitcom group. Special thanks to Harris Cohen and everyone at the Sound Bite Institute: Chuck, Kiki, Vera, Mohammed, Big Dave, Little Dave, and Morty.

And most thanks to my parents, Mom and Dad, who supported me until I was twenty-one and encouraged me every day since.

INTRODUCTION

It is a good thing for an uneducated man to read a book of quotations.

—Winston Churchill

Not this one. *"I Am Not a Corpse!"* is a quote book that attempts to fill a much-needed void: the chasm between fact and fiction. It is history and culture, disingenuous and misinformed.

This is the book that strives to uneducate the great washed.

Katz, Mark
New York, N.Y.

Aaron

MOSES' YOUNGER BROTHER

Moses this. Moses that.
Moses! Moses! Moses!

Abdul Mejid

EMPEROR OF OTTOMAN EMPIRE

Bring me something upon which I may rest my weary feet.

Abraham

INVENTOR OF MONOTHEISM

Isaac, this is going to hurt you more than it's going to hurt me.
—the first circumcision

Achilles

MYTHOLOGICAL WARRIOR

Do you have this in a high-top?
—inquiry to sandal clerk

Adam

FIRST MAN

No, no! I asked you to bring me back a Snapple!

——

I think we should see other people.

—breaking up with Eve

Agnew, Spiro

FORMER U.S. VICE PRESIDENT

I regret that I was unable to maintain the ethical standards of the Nixon administration.

—letter of resignation

Aldrin, Eugene (Buzz)

SECOND MAN ON THE MOON

Tails.

Alexander the Great

CONQUEROR OF PERSIAN EMPIRE

I'd like you to meet my brothers, Stan the Entirely Adequate and Mort the Well-Above-Average.

Ames, Aldrich

MASTER SPY

Ello-hay oviets-say. It's ick-ray. I ant-way my ayment-pay.
> —secret coded communications made from his office desk

Andersen, Hans Christian
WRITER OF CHILDREN'S STORIES

"The Magical Reappearing Sore"
"The Lonely Shepherd"
"Gretta Has Two Mommies"
—unpublished works

Andretti, Mario
RACE CAR DRIVER

Why, yes, officer. I do think I'm Mario Andretti.
—frequent response to state troopers

Anthony, Susan B.

PIONEER FEMINIST

Babe

—what the "B" stands for

Arafat, Yasir

PLO LEADER

> *You don't have to be Jewish to love Levy's Jewish Rye!*
> —breakthrough peace treaty concession, 1994

> *I'm so happy, I could blow up a bus.*
> —accepting Nobel Peace prize, 1994

Aristophanes

GREEK COMEDY WRITER

*I just came in from Sparta.
Boy, are my legs tired!*

Armstrong, Neil

U.S. ASTRONAUT

*Houston. This is Eagle. Are we
there yet?*
> —question repeated incessantly

*How come we can put a man on
the moon but we can't invent a
decent orange-flavored instant
beverage?*

Arthur, Chester A.

TWENTY-FIRST U.S. PRESIDENT

Peace. Prosperity. Muttonchops.
  —unsuccessful reelection slogan, 1886

Attila the Hun

SIXTH-CENTURY EUROPEAN MARAUDER

*By the time I'm through, no one
will remember the name
"Trepkor the Hun."*
> —vowing to exceed the carnage
> of his predecessor

*Do these shoes go with this
helmet?*
> —preparing to invade France

*Gentlemen, gentlemen—
this is a looting, not a massacre.
Let's act civilized.*
> —restoring order to his troops

Avogadro, Amadeo

MOLECULAR PHYSICIST

602-1023
> —Avogadro's Telephone Number

Bacchus

ROMAN GOD OF WINE AND REVELRY

Hello, my name is Bacchus—
and I'm an alcoholic.

Bach, Johann Sebastian

CLASSICAL COMPOSER

Bach Unfugued

—best-selling CD

Bakker, Rev. Jim

EVANGELICAL FELON

*Praise the Lord and pass the
scented body oils!*
>—remark to Jessica Hahn

*The missionary position? Never
heard of it.*
>—ibid.

Bannister, Roger

RUNNER

*And now I will hard-boil an egg
in under three minutes.*
>—announcing his second record-
breaking endeavor

Baptist, John the

EARLY CHRISTIAN

Rinse. Repeat if necessary.

Barnum, P. T.

SHOWMAN

That's no bearded lady.
That's my wife!

Barry, Marion

MAYOR, WASHINGTON, D.C.

I will stop returning their phone
calls.

—campaign pledge to get tough
on drug dealers, 1994

Beethoven, Ludwig van
COMPOSER

I never listen to critics.

Bell, Alexander Graham
SCIENTIST AND INVENTOR

*Mr. Watson. Come here.
I want you. Bad!*
—inventing phone sex

Bennett, Tony
SINGER

*Say, any of you youngsters want
to have a rap session?*
—hosting *MTV Beach House*

Berra, Lawrence (Yogi)

BASEBALL PLAYER

Surely you jest. These so-called "Yogisms" are archetypal examples of absurdist non sequiturs.

—denying authorship

Birdseye, Clarence

FOOD PIONEER

*I wish to be frozen in a
light cream sauce.*
—last will and testament

Bloomfeld, Harry, D.D.S.

RENEGADE DENTIST

I recommend sugared *gum for
my patients who chew gum.*
—sole dissenter among five for chewing-
gum questionnaire

Bozo

TELEVISION CLOWN

No Geraldos!

—lapel pin

Do you have these in a forty-two and a half?

—inquiry to shoe clerk

Bond, James
BRITISH SECRET AGENT

I'd like to apply for a permit to kill.

—age sixteen

Booth, John Wilkes
ACTOR/ASSASSIN

Did they mention me in the reviews?

—the next day

Boyardee, Chef
PURVEYOR OF CANNED GOODS

With the SpaghettiOs, I'd recommend something with more body. I have a precocious Fruit Juicy Red 1982.

Brando, Marlon
ACTOR

One day, I'm gonna be bigger than Orson Welles.

—career prediction

Braun, Eva

MRS. ADOLF HITLER

I can't stand his moustache, but I don't dare tell him.
> —secret diary

Sorry we couldn't invite you to the wedding, but it was a very small bunker.
> —letter to close friends and relatives

Brezhnev, Leonid

SOVIET LEADER

Does this gray tie go with this gray suit?
> —picking out daily outfit

Buchanan, Pat

GOP PRESIDENTIAL CANDIDATE

Mein Kampaign
> —1992 convention speech

Buckley, William F.
CONSERVATIVE COMMENTATOR

Def Master fud-E-dud
—street name

Burns, Ken
FILMMAKER

Baseball's Civil War: The History of the Designated Hitter Rule
—original proposal to PBS

Burton, Richard
ACTOR

Darling, is that all you're eating?
—at dinner with fiancée Liz Taylor

Why don't you have a salad, dear?
—at dinner with wife Liz Taylor

Bush, George H. W.

FORTY-FIRST U.S. PRESIDENT

I'ya, you betcha—well heck yeah!—sure do.
—marriage vow to wife Barbara

*Fascinating. You say someday
these "VCRs" will be available
to ordinary Americans?*
—campaign trail, 1992

Buttafuoco, Joey

STAR-CROSSED LOVER

We'll always have Massapequa.
—poignant farewell with Amy Fisher

see also: Fisher, Amy

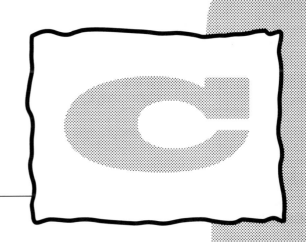

Caesar, Julius
ROMAN EMPEROR

Pizza! Pizza!

—first words

Okay, one more time. What do I do when I get to the Rubicon?

—pulling over for directions on his way back from Gaul

No anchovies!

—ordering salad

Caligula

LIBERTINE ROMAN EMPEROR

Veni. Veni. Veni.

Camel, Joe

ANIMATED SMOKING ADVOCATE

Larry Lead Paint Chip
''Airplane Glue'' Jack
Ricky Runwithscissors

—other aliases

Capone, Al

GANGSTER

*Reward your friends, punish
your enemies, and save your
receipts.*

> —advice to Al Jr.

Carson, Johnny
TALK-SHOW KING EMERITUS

For chrissake, Ed, have a breath mint.

Carter, Jimmy

THIRTY-NINTH U.S. PRESIDENT

*At the request of the White House,
I am on my way to resolve the
crisis in hell.*
—press conference, 1995

Casanova

LEGENDARY LOVER

*I'll have a pack of ribbed Trojans,
a tube of K-Y jelly—family size—
vitamin E supplements . . . oh,
and uh, uh, a bottle of Head & Shoulders.*
—awkward teenage moment
in a drugstore

Castro, Fidel

CUBAN DICTATOR

Close but no cigar.
> —telegram to JFK following Bay
> of Pigs invasion

Chamberlain, Wilt

BASKETBALL LEGEND

Roses are red,
Violets are blue.
Happy Valentine's Day
 # 9072

Chanel, Coco

FASHION ENTREPRENEUR

Perfume No. 4 smells like goat cheese. Must keep trying.
—diary entry, 1919

Charles, Prince

ASPIRING MONARCH

The geek formerly known as Prince
—future title

Child, Julia

TELEVISION GOURMET

> *Of course, for those preparing this dish at home, fresh pâté is preferable to pureed Spam.*
> —making do with PBS cutbacks

Christ, Jesus

FOUNDER OF CHRISTIANITY

> *I'm sorry, Luke, I didn't know you were serving fish. I'll just turn it into a sauvignon blanc.*
> —showing up at the Last Supper

> *I will be bigger than the Beatles.*
> —John 5:8

Chung, Connie

TV JOURNALIST

Larry King and Connie Chung Live!
Regis, Connie & Kathy Lee
Ringling Brothers Connie Chung Barnum & Bailey Circus
Dionne Warwick's & Connie Chung's Psychic Friends Network
—job prospects

Churchill, Winston

BRITISH PRIME MINISTER

Can you get blood, toil, tears, and sweat out of this shirt?
—inquiry to dry cleaner

Clark, Dick

TELEVISION PERSONALITY

For chrissake, Ed, have a breath mint.

Claus, Santa

CHRISTMAS COURIER

Yeah right. And I'm Santa Claus.
—meeting the Easter Bunny

I wish I had a present for you, Timmy, but I'm afraid I just don't believe in little boys.
—favorite taunt

Clinton, Hillary Rodham

FIRST LADY

When I speak, E. F. Hutton listens.

Clinton, William Jefferson (Bill)

FORTY-SECOND U.S. PRESIDENT

You gonna finish that?
—remark to Jacques Chirac, state dinner

No shirt. No shoes. No service.
—fallback position on controversial
military personnel policy

Cochran, Johnnie

DEFENSE ATTORNEY

Honey, I know I'm late for dinner, but I have a very plausible alibi.

Columbus, Christopher

EXPLORER

We'll have the chicken tandoori, curried rice, and a vegetable samosa.

—odd remark to the natives of San Salvador

Confucius

PHILOSOPHER

An enigma wrapped inside a conundrum baked inside a tasty lemony crust.

—recipe for fortune cookie

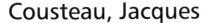

Cousteau, Jacques

OCEANOGRAPHER

Retournez le bateau!
Tu as oublié d'apporter
la sauce tartare,
espèce d'idiot!
　　—translation: Turn back the vessel! You
forgot to pack the tartar sauce, you idiot!

Cowlings, Al

O.J. LACKEY

O.J., do you want a receipt?
　　—tollbooth, Santa Monica Freeway

Crunch, Cap'n
CEREAL-LOVING SEAMAN

> *Land ho!*
> *Prepare to go ashore*
> *for fresh milk and*
> *crunchberries, mateys!*

cummings, e.e.
POET

> *if only i—*
> *could sell acouple*
> *of lousy p-o-e-m-s;*
> *,i could afford*
> *toget this (damn)*
> *typewriter fixed.*

Daguerre, Louis
INVENTOR OF PHOTOGRAPHY

Say "Gruyere!"

Dali, Salvador
PAINTER

You like me! You surreally like me!
—accepting the coveted "Brushy" award

D'Amato, Alfonse
U.S. SENATOR

That which does not convict me only makes me stronger.

Darrow, Clarence S.
DEFENSE ATTORNEY

Your Honor, I call to the witness stand Mr. Magilla Gorilla.
—announcing surprise witness at the Scopes monkey trial

Darwin, Charles
SCIENTIFIC THEORIST

Exhibit A
—cruel nickname for his brother Fred

da Vinci, Leonardo

PAINTER/SCULPTOR/SCIENTIST/INVENTOR

Big deal. These days, everyone is a Renaissance man.

Davis, Jefferson

CONFEDERATE PRESIDENT

Forget Iowa and New Hampshire. I'm counting on Super Tuesday.
—presidential campaign strategy, 1864

de Gaulle, Charles

FRENCH PRIME MINISTER

*Okay, here's the plan.
If we act rude enough,
maybe the Nazis will just go home.*
—radio address, 1939

49

Dershowitz, Alan

DEFENSE ATTORNEY

*A man is presumed innocent
until proven insane.*

---

*Character references:
Mike Tyson, O. J. Simpson,
Claus von Bulow*

—curriculum vitae

Descartes, René

THEORIST

I'm dead. Therefore I'm not.

—logical epitaph

Dewey, Melvil

LIBRARIAN

0–10	heavy jacket
10–20	warm sweater
20–30	windbreaker (optional)
30–40	double-knit slacks
50–60	shorts and T-shirt
60–70	anything mesh
70–80	talcum powder
80–90	mosquito netting
90–100	Solarcaine

—the Dewey Centigrade System

Donaldson, Sam

TELEVISION JOURNALIST

Live long and prosper.

Dole, Robert
SENATE MAJORITY LEADER

Hey, you kids! Get off my lawn!

I've fallen, and I can get up!
—TV spot dispelling the age issue

Dorothy
SHE OF THE RUBY SLIPPERS

I'm originally from Kansas, but most of my friends live in the West Village.

Dracula, Count

VAMPIRE

> *Help yourself to some cookies and orange juice.*
> —frequent offer to houseguests

Dukakis, Michael S.

1988 DEMOCRATIC PRESIDENTIAL CANDIDATE

> *I have not yet begun to fight.*
> —concession speech, 1988

Earhart, Amelia

AVIATOR

This is the last flight I take with a layover.

Ebert, Roger

MOVIE CRITIC

No, Mom, it's me—Ebert. Siskel's the bald one.

Ebert   Siskel

Eisenhower, Dwight D.

THIRTY-FOURTH U.S. PRESIDENT

If South Vietnam falls to the Communists,
so will Laos, then Thailand.
Next thing you know,
they'll be delivering pizzas all
over Southeast Asia
within thirty minutes.
—explaining the Domino's theory

Einstein, Albert

THEORETICAL PHYSICIST

I realized I was blessed with above-average intelligence when classmates began referring to me as "Einstein."

———

$$9.7R\,\frac{(Y\,K)}{G} \geq \Omega\pi \times 10^{11}$$

—locker combination

———

You press down this little button and—vonderbar!—the garage door opens by itself!!!

—last contribution to science

Elders, Joycelyn

FORMER U.S. SURGEON GENERAL

How could he fire me? I was his right hand.

Elizabeth

QUEEN OF ENGLAND

You're not exactly a prince.
—pressuring Charles into marriage

Eve

FIRST WOMAN

Four inches! That's huge!
—easily impressed

Fay, Michael

CANING VICTIM

I was sentenced to six strokes.
But my lawyer took a third.

> —explaining his reduced sentence,
> *Larry King Live*

Fisher, Amy

STAR-CROSSED LOVER

Play it, Sam.
Play "Like a Virgin."

see also: Buttafuoco, Joey

Fletcher, Jessica

TELEVISION DETECTIVE, *MURDER, SHE WROTE*

Every week I visit another friend.
Every week there's another corpse.
Every week I pin the rap on another idiot.
I can't believe it took you
imbeciles so long to catch on.
—confession to authorities, series finale

Fonda, Jane

ACTRESS/ACTIVIST/AEROBICIST

Hey hey, LBJ!
How many squat thrusts
have you done today?

Forbes, Malcolm "Steve"

ANGRY AFFLUENT

I'm rich as hell and I'm not gonna take it anymore.

Ford, Gerald R.

THIRTY-EIGHTH U.S. PRESIDENT

Who resigned and made you president?
> —keeping Henry Kissinger in line

Ford, Betty
FORMER FIRST LADY

> *The viability of this clinic depends on attracting repeat customers.*
>
> —business development plan

Ford, Henry
INDUSTRIALIST

> *Quantity is Job 1.*
>
> —opening ceremonies, first production line

Fortensky, Elizabeth Taylor Hilton Wilding Todd Fisher Burton Burton Warner
DIVA

> *Michael Jackson is the sanest person I know.*
>
> —character witness
>
> *see also: Jackson, Michael*

Francis of Assisi
SAINT

Who are you calling Assisi?

Franklin, Benjamin
STATESMAN/SCIENTIST/AUTHOR

*Asparagus smells delicious at dinner
and curious by dawn.*

*Out all night, asleep by noon;
you're in rehab pretty soon.*

*The man who keeps a dog never
has to admit to his own flatulence.*
—rejected aphorisms

Freud, Sigmund
PSYCHOANALYST

*I'm tired, Smother. I'm going
back to my womb.*

——

*Your superego says "no, no, no"
but your id says "yes, yes, yes."*
—pickup line

Fuhrman, Mark
FORMER L.A. DETECTIVE

Nuts.
Neanderthal.
Neo-Nazi.
Nolo contendere.
—appropriate "N-words"

G., Kenny
MUSICIAN

Garfunkel
—what the "G" stands for

Gandhi, Mahatma
INDIAN NATIONALIST LEADER

Yes, I'd like to order the lamb vindaloo
for delivery. My name?
Uhh . . . Gordon.
—secret telephone conversation

Garcia, Jerry

MUSICIAN

Chunky Junkie

—second ice cream flavor
named in his honor

Gates, Bill

MICROSOFT MOGUL

When you've got them by the software,
their hearts and minds will follow.

Gates, Daryl
FORMER LAPD COMMISSIONER

You have the right to remain handcuffed.
This billy club can and will be used against you.

George III
BRITISH KING

Taxation without
representation.
—campaign slogan, 1760

Geraldo!

SERIOUS JOURNALIST

Hey, you're looking at the guy who put the ''cheese'' in machismo!

Ghali, Boutros Boutros-

UN SECRETARY-GENERAL

Boutros-Boutros Dolly
—his other life

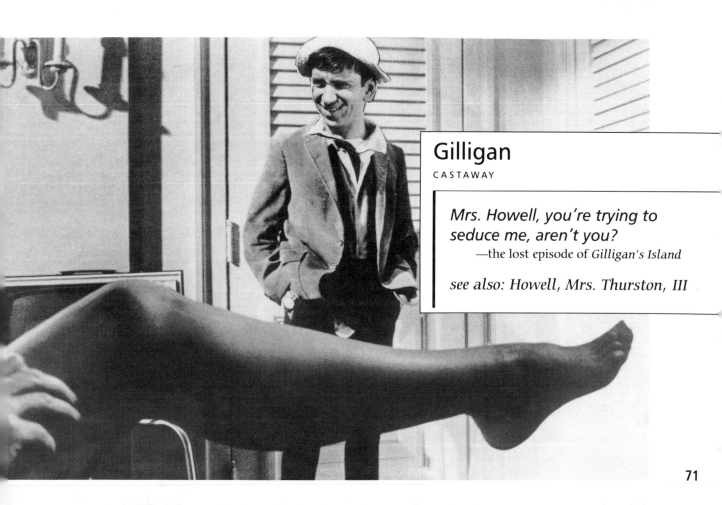

Gilligan
CASTAWAY

Mrs. Howell, you're trying to seduce me, aren't you?
—the lost episode of *Gilligan's Island*

see also: Howell, Mrs. Thurston, III

Gilooly, Jeff

GOON HIRER

While there is a lower class, I am in it. While there is a criminal element, I am of it. While there is a soul in prison, I am not free.
                          —sentencing hearing

Ginger

CASTAWAY

Mrs. Howell! Are you trying to get me drunk??
         —the lost episode of *Gilligan's Island*

see also: Howell, Mrs. Thurston, III

Gingrich, Newt
OVERZEALOUS SPEAKER

I think it's high time we took a closer look into the living arrangements of Bert and Ernie.
—House PBS hearings, 1995

Contract with Canada
Contract with Mexico
Contract with France
—to-do list

God
OMNIPOTENT BEING

. . . I said, "Let there be light!"
—experiencing technical difficulties

C'mon, seven!
—playing dice with the universe

Godiva, Lady
PROVOCATIVE TAX PROTESTER

Read my lips: no new taxes.

Godot
EXISTENTIAL ENIGMA

Back in five minutes.

Gorbachev, Mikhail
SOVIET LEADER

How many ICM missiles do you want for a pair of Levi 501's?
—Reykjavik summit negotiations

Gore, Al

U.S. VICE PRESIDENT

"Sexiest Man Ostensibly Alive, 1992"

—*People* magazine

Gramm, Phil

U.S. SENATOR

Show me the candidate more committed to the rights of gun owners than me, and I'll shoot him.

—flanking to the right

Grant, Hugh
NAUGHTY MOVIE STAR

> *I'm looking for something with tinted windows and lots of headroom.*
>
> —replacing the Beemer

Gutenberg, Johann
INVENTOR, PRINTING PRESS

> *Thank you for your manuscript, but it does not meet our current needs.*
>
> —first form letter

Hammurabi
KING OF BABYLONIA

Don't even think of parking here.
—The Code, Part IV, sec. 6(a):
Regulations, Parking and Traffic

Hancock, John
AMERICAN PATRIOT

Lookie here, Jefferson. I'm writing my name in the snow.

Heimlich, Dr. Henry J.

INVENTOR, HEIMLICH MANEUVER

> *Team Doctor of the Buffalo Bills*
> —official title

Helms, Jesse

U.S. SENATOR

> *Come to the dark side, Newt. Together, we shall rule the galaxy.*
> —election night, 1994

Henry VIII
KING OF ENGLAND

My wife is separated.
—explaining his marital status

Henry, Patrick

U.S. PATRIOT

> . . . *but if it's all the same to you,*
> *I'd prefer liberty.*
>
> —afterthought

Herzl, Theodor

ZIONIST

> *I am a Hebrew Nationalist. I*
> *answer to a higher authority.*
>
> —address to League of Nations

Hess, Rudolf

NAZI WAR CRIMINAL

I was only giving orders.
—unsuccessful Nuremberg defense

Hippocrates
FIRST PHYSICIAN

No, seriously. I call it "gynecology."
—trying to convince reluctant women of
his newfound specialty

Hitler, Adolf
FÜHRER

See evil. Hear evil. Do evil.

—

Visualize World Domination
—bumper sticker

Hood, Robin

LEGENDARY WOODSMAN

So you want to join my Merry Men? Are you aware of the initiation ceremony?
—interviewing new recruit

Hoover, J. Edgar

FBI DIRECTOR

I always get my man.

Howell, Mrs. Thurston, III

CASTAWAY

Please, call me "Lovey."
—the lost episode of *Gilligan's Island*

Howell, Thurston, III

CASTAWAY

Ginger darling, as soon as we get off this damn island, I'll divorce the old girl and we'll be married! Won't that be just splendid?
—the lost episode of *Gilligan's Island*

Hudson, Henry
NEW WORLD EXPLORER

> *Hey, no! No!*
> *My windshields are clean.*
> *I said . . . . aww shit.*
>> —arriving in New York harbor

Hun, Attila the   *see Attila the Hun*

Hussein, Saddam

IRAQI DICTATOR

Hello, Allstate?

—January 1991

Isabella

QUEEN OF SPAIN

Columbus went to the New World, and all I got was this lousy T-shirt!

——

A crueler, more gentile nation
   —announcing the Spanish Inquisition,
1492

Ito, Lance

JUDGE

> *I will remind the witness again*
> *not to address me as "Mr. Sulu."*
> —reprimanding Kato Kaelin

Jackson, Jesse L.

POLITICAL ACTIVIST

Crime is bad,
Bosnia's messy.
Don't be sad,
Vote for Jesse.
> —campaign 1996 position paper

Jackson, Michael

KING OF POP

> *Would you like to come with me to Never-Never-Tell Land?*

> *Some of my best defense attorneys are Jewish.*
> —dismissing accusations of anti-Semitism

> *Liz Taylor is the sanest person I know.*
> —character reference

see also: Fortensky, Elizabeth Taylor

Jefferson, Thomas

THIRD U.S. PRESIDENT

Throw in a dozen of those delicious flaky pastries, and you've got yourself a deal!
—concluding the Louisiana Purchase

You think Zoë Baird *had a nanny problem?*

Jennings, Peter

NEWS ANCHOR

See you real soon!
—Disney/*ABC Evening News* sign-off

Joan of Arc

CHRISTIAN SAINT AND MARTYR

I'm just going to hand out a couple of pamphlets. What's the worst they can possibly do to me?

Job

LONG-SUFFERING BELIEVER

Let's go Cubs!

Jobs, Steven
FOUNDER, APPLE COMPUTERS

I 🍎 *-Q.*

—letter of resignation

Joel, Billy
PIANO MAN

Pls. cancel my subscription to Sports Illustrated.

John Paul II, Pope
PONTIFF

What do you a mean, ''second draft''?
Just print what I gave you.
I'm infallible, for Christ's sake!

—conversation with book editor

What's today, Friday? I'll have the Filet-O-Fish.

Johnson, Lyndon

THIRTY-SIXTH U.S. PRESIDENT

No more of that damn chowder in the White House mess!
>—first official act as president

The next person who says "quagmire" gets a punch in the face.
>—meeting with Joint Chiefs of Staff

Kaelin, Kato

MALE BIMBO

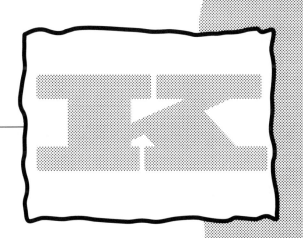

Situation wanted: nonsmoking freeloader seeks celeb w/guest house & pool. Willing to testify.

Kennedy, Edward M. (Ted)

U.S. SENATOR

Mother, when do I get to be president?

—adolescent gripe

Kennedy, John Fitzgerald

THIRTY-FIFTH U.S. PRESIDENT

I got so plastered last night, I went home with some broad who looked like J. Edgar Hoover.
—confession to Secret Service agent

I know it's a lot of crap, Bobby. The only missile gap is the one in Dick Nixon's pants.
—following 1960 presidential debate

It's not that I don't find you attractive, but my father wouldn't approve.
—letting Golda Meir down easy

Kennedy, John, Jr.

SEXIEST PUBLISHER ALIVE

Hi.

—surefire pickup line

Kevorkian, Jack

SUICIDE DOCTOR

Today is the last day of the rest of your life.
>—inspirational waiting room sign

Call now and be dead by Christmas! Guaranteed.
>—holiday season promotion

Key, Francis Scott

COMPOSER, ''THE STAR-SPANGLED BANNER''

Hey, it beats "Yankee Doodle"!
>—main selling point

Keynes, John Maynard
ECONOMIC THEORIST

I could have had a V-8!
—discovering "opportunity costs"

Khomeini, Ayatollah
IRANIAN THEO-DICTATOR

Extremism in defense of extremism is no vice!
—despot nominating convention,
Teheran, 1972

Kid, Billy the
OUTLAW

Your Honor, I just assumed I'd be tried as a minor.

King, Larry

INTERVIEWER

Caller, what's the question?
—answering machine message

King, Martin Luther, Jr.

CIVIL RIGHTS LEADER

The food is lousy in here.
—postcard from Birmingham Jail

King, Stephen

HORROR NOVELIST

*Please excuse my son from gym today.
His body and soul have been possessed by a
satanic force unleashed by a disturbance in a
local tribal burial ground.*

Kinsey, Alfred

SEXUAL BEHAVIORIST

*Psst. Down here. Under the bed.
Mind if I ask you two a few
questions?*

Kirk, Captain James T.
STAR FLEET COMMANDER

I'm not only captain of the U.S.S. Enterprise.
I'm also a client.

Kissinger, Henry
GLOBAL PLAYER

''Ich bin ein Berliner.'' *Brilliant!*
Why didn't I think of that?

Klein, Calvin
FASHION DESIGNER

Screw you and the horse you
rode in on.
—nasty words for Ralph Lauren

Knievel, Evel

DAREDEVIL

*What, are you crazy? I got a
wife and kids.*
>—refusing to fly on USAir

Koop, C. Everett

FORMER SURGEON GENERAL

*Also avoid inhaling secondhand
Vicks VapoRub.*
>—surgeon general's report, 1987

Koresh, David

HOMICIDAL CULT LEADER

Am I crazy, or is it hot in here?

Kreskin, The Amazing

MENTALIST

Joyce, I can name that tune in no notes.

—game-show appearance

Kuralt, Charles

TELEVISION JOURNALIST

1.6 billion miles @ 25¢/mi = $40,000,000

—final expense report

Laffer, Arthur

SUPPLY-SIDE ECONOMIST

How to Lose Weight on
12,000 Calories a Day
—subtitle of *The Supply-Side Diet Book*

Leary, Timothy

DRUG ADVOCATE

*When I bite into a York
Peppermint Patty, I get the
sensation that I'm floating on
a bowl of tangerine Jell-O,
as marsupial nymphs cleanse
my soul with moist towelettes.*

Lee, Robert E.

CONFEDERATE GENERAL

> *We still get to drawl and chew tobacky, right?*
> —conditions for surrender

Lewis, Meriwether

FRONTIER EXPLORER

> *I thought* you *packed the sandwiches!*
> —first night on the trail with Clark

Liberty, Lady
STATUESQUE WOMAN

> *The only guys I ever meet are tired, wretched, or poor.*

Lincoln, Abraham
SIXTEENTH U.S. PRESIDENT

*Going back around—oh, I'd say—
eighty-five years or so . . .*
—first draft of Gettysburg Address

Lindbergh, Charles A.
AVIATION HERO

000-000-001
—Frequent Flyer number

Locke, John
POLITICAL THEORIST

Some tabulas are more rasa than others.
—dismissing the criticism of Rousseau

Lucci, Susan
DAYTIME TELEVISION ACTRESS

Thanks for nothing, you bastards.
—acceptance speech she carries with her to Emmy awards

MacArthur, Douglas

WWII GENERAL

Old soldiers die.

—postdenial

Machiavelli, Niccolò

POLITICAL THEORIST

> *You won't have Nick Machiavelli to kick around anymore.*
> —last press conference, 1521

Madonna

MATERIAL GIRL

> *McDonna*
> —*really* selling out

Manilow, Barry
SAPPY SINGER

Even I hate Michael Bolton.

Manson, Charles
HOMICIDAL MANIAC

If I'm not rehabilitated enough to be placed back into society, how 'bout the National Hockey League?

—parole board hearings

Marceau, Marcel

MIME ARTIST

Marconi, Guglielmo

INVENTOR OF RADIO

And now our first caller,
Mr. Alexander Graham Bell.
—inventing the radio call-in program

Marcos, Imelda

DISGRACED FILIPINO POLITICIAN AND SOCIALITE

Angry mobs surround palace
demanding my execution. . . .
Desperate. My world is
collapsing. . . . Negotiating
refuge in Hawaii. . . . Will need
new sandals.
—diary entry, 1981

Marshall, George C.

FORMER U.S. SECRETARY OF STATE

Finally, if the $40 billion in financial aid doesn't get Europe back on its feet, we can put up a huge Disney theme park in the middle of France. (Just kidding.)

—memo to Truman outlining
the Marshall Plan

Marx, Karl

MARXIST

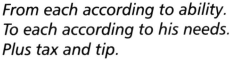

From each according to ability.
To each according to his needs.
Plus tax and tip.

—splitting the bill with friends
at a restaurant

Don't give me that "communal
property" shit. The stereo is
mine!

—messy divorce settlement

Maryanne

CASTAWAY

Well, Mrs. Howell, I have to
admit I'm flattered, maybe even
a little bit curious, but . . .

—the lost episode of *Gilligan's Island*

see also: Howell, Mrs. Thurston, III

Mayer, Oscar

LUNCH MEAT VENDOR

> *My salami has a first name.*
> *It's "Mister Happy."*
>
> —crude remark

McCarthy, Joseph

ANTI-COMMUNIST SENATOR

> *And Mr. Kozlowski, can you tell*
> *us the name of the baseball*
> *team you play for in Cincinnati?*
>
> —hearings on the infiltration of
> Communists into professional sports

McLaughlin, John
POLITICAL PUNDIT

*Issue one: my impossibly
affected demeanor.
Mor-ton! . . .*

Mendel, Gregor
GENETICIST/MONK

*I chose the celibate life of
a monk because if I were to
have a child, there was a 25%
chance it would be a short
yellow pea.*

—confused by the ramifications
of his own experiments

117

Michelangelo

PAINTER/SCULPTOR

> *Your Holiness, nobody said anything to me about using a dropcloth.*

Miranda, Carmen

LATIN MOVIE STAR

> *Never wear mango after Labor Day.*

Molotov, Vyacheslav

SOVIET REVOLUTIONARY LEADER

Pffftuuuuu! This tastes like gasoline!
> —tasting drink prepared in his honor

Mondale, Walter

1984 DEMOCRATIC PRESIDENTIAL CANDIDATE

As goes Massachusetts, so goes the District of Columbia.
> —election night prophecy

Monroe, Marilyn

ACTRESS/ICON

Oh, okay. I'll baby-sit for Teddy.

Montana, Joe

LEGENDARY QUARTERBACK

> *If I hear "It's a Small World After All"*
> *one more time, I'm gonna strangle*
> *one of those stupid midgets.*
> —winning one too many Super Bowls

Morse, Samuel F. B.

INVENTOR

> — . — . . .
> . . . . . .
> — . — — . .
> — . . — . .
> . .
> —last words (translation: CHEST PAINS!)

Moses

I know exactly where we are.
>—after thirty-eight years
>lost in the desert

Mozart, Wolfgang Amadeus

COMPOSER

*"Tonight We're Gonna Party
Like It's 1799"*
>—hit single

Mussolini, Benito

FASCIST

I torture! I massacre! I have plans for world domination! How come Hitler gets all the bad press?
　—chewing out his press secretary, 1941

Napoleon

FRENCH CONQUEROR

*Curse that Count de Custarde!
I must invent a dessert of
my own!*

Newton, Sir Isaac

SCIENTIST

> *I was resting beneath a tree when a fig fell on my head. And then I started wondering . . .*
> —how he invented the Fig Newton

Nixon, Richard Milhous

THIRTY-SEVENTH U.S. PRESIDENT

Liddy, while you're at it, break into a 7-Eleven and bring me back a burrito and Sprite Big Gulp.

———

Well, Sirica can expletive deleted himself. I'll do whatever the expletive deleted I want. I'm the expletive deleted president!
—verbatim transcript

———

I am not a corpse.
—tombstone inscription

Nobel, Alfred

CHEMIST

Whaddya want? A medal?
>—nasty remark to lab clerk

Nostradamus

FIFTEENTH-CENTURY ASTROLOGER

In the twentieth century in the year of our Lord, a tribe of ransackers will triumph over swarming birds of prey.
>—predicting the winner of Super Bowl XV (Raiders 27, Eagles 10)

Oedipus
GREEK KING

I just can't seem to find the right Hallmark card.
> —annual Mother's Day quandary

Ono, Yoko
WIFE OF JOHN LENNON

We *are the walrus.*

Oppenheimer, J. Robert

FATHER OF THE ATOMIC BOMB

> *(plutonium 386)* $\times$ *mc^2* =
> *KABLOOIE!!*
> —second postulate of relativity theory

Oswald, Lee Harvey

ASSASSIN

> *I am the NRA.*

Packwood, Robert

U.S. SENATOR

Hands-on Washington experience.

—reelection campaign slogan

Pasteur, Louis

BIOLOGIST

I have read the mad, mad essays of Dr. Pierre Homogen. Ha! As if milk could be improved upon yet again!

—letter to the editor, *England Journal of Medicine*

Pavlov, Ivan
BEHAVIORAL SCIENTIST

Please knock. DON'T RING BELL*!*
—posted sign

Perdue, Frank
POULTRY KING

Okay, who's the wiseguy who plucked my head?

Perot, H. Ross

ILLIONAIRE POPULIST

Now, I don't wanna do it, but if all my supporters in all fifty states go out and get petitions signed, I'd be willing to seek professional psychiatric help.
　　　　　　　　—Larry King Live

——

I'll take "Things That Make Sucking Sounds" for $100, Alex.
　　　　　　　　—Crackpot Week on *Jeopardy!*

Plato

PHILOSOPHER

No, Ma. We're just good friends.

Post, Emily
ETIQUETTE EXPERT

I tried being polite, but obviously that doesn't work. Now, quit calling me, you sonsabitches!!

—refusing to switch her
long-distance service

Powell, Colin
RELUCTANT WARRIOR

. . . And Mario Cuomo has agreed not to be my running mate.

—noncandidacy speech, 1995

Powers, J. D.
CONSUMER SATISFACTION GURU

On a scale of 1 to 5—with 1 being a thoroughly degrading experience and 5 being the fulfillment of your wildest fantasies—how was it for you?

Presley, Elvis Aaron
KING OF ROCK 'N' ROLL

FOOD, DRUGS & ROCK 'N' ROLL!

Professor, the
CASTAWAY

I have needs too, Mrs. Howell. I need to get out of your hut before Mr. Howell gets back!
　　—the lost episode of *Gilligan's Island*

see also: Howell, Mrs. Thurston, III

Prynne, Hester

ADULTERESS, *THE SCARLET LETTER*

> *They should make him wear a C-minus.*
>
> —complaining about her lover, the
> Reverend Arthur Dimmesdale

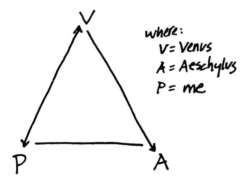

where:
V = Venus
A = Aeschylus
P = me

Pythagoras

INVENTOR OF THE TRIANGLE

> *I love Venus. Venus loves me. But she also loves Aeschylus. It's complicated, but I've figured out how it can work.*

Quayle, Dan

FORMER VICE PRESIDENT

It doesn't help matters when Charlie Brown just hangs around the 'hood with Linus, Lucy, and Schroeder without any sign of parental supervision. Is it any wonder that they are still in elementary school after all these years?

—espousing family values in his famous "Charlie Brown" speech

And how did I do?

—awkward moment, election night 1992

Queeg, Captain

COMMANDER, U.S.S. *CAINE*

No. Isaac was too busy conspiring with Julie. I think it was Gopher who stole my strawberries.

—guest appearance on *The Love Boat*

Raleigh, Sir Walter

COLONIAL SETTLER

There is no scientific evidence that conclusively proves that I invented cigarettes.

　　　　　—congressional testimony

Rand, Ayn
LIBERTARIAN CULT LEADER

Greed is good.

Reagan, Ronald
FORTIETH U.S. PRESIDENT

Let me see if I understand this correctly: The government is spending more jelly beans than we have in the jar.
> —economic briefing with
> David Stockman

Reed, Ralph
CHRISTIAN POWER BROKER

Newt, gotta go. I got God on the other line.

Revere, Paul
PATRIOTIC ALARMIST

This is a test of the Emergency Broadcast System!

Richards, Keith
ROCK 'N' ROLL MUSICIAN

Dress young, and live in a good-looking corpse.

Ripken, Cal
PERSISTENCE PERSONIFIED

It takes 7,214 licks to get to the center of a Tootsie Pop.

Rizzuto, Phil "Scooter"

N.Y. YANKEE ANNOUNCER

Talk about tiramisu! Cora and I were out to dinner over at Dom Badami's new restaurant over in Hackensack. I mean, rich! White, do you eat that tiramisu? Ooh boy, I'm telling you. Tiramisu. Cannoli. Biscotti. Cora loves biscotti. If I don't hit too much traffic going over the bridge tonight, we're going to Tony Roma's new place in Teaneck. They got some kind of ribs there. Mmm! Although the last time I had ribs, I cracked a filling in my tooth and had to have all kinds of dental work done. Dr. Carmine Capprizzi over in East Brunswick. And his son, Carmine Jr. Just broke 200 bowling the other night! Ever crack a filling, White? Ouch! . . . Hey! Did I mention today is Sal Maglie's birthday?

—calling final out of the 1977 World Series

Robert
PARLIAMENTARIAN

SHUT UP! SHUT UP! SHUT THE HELL UP!
JUST SHUT UP!
> —incident prior to his Rules of Order

Roberts, Julia
PRETTY ACTRESS

Lyle, why the long face?

Robespierre, Maximilien de
FRENCH REVOLUTIONARY LEADER

I may disagree with what you say,
but I'll defend to your death
my right to kill you.

Robin

BOY WONDER

Stephanopoulos

—last name

Robinson, Jackie
BASEBALL PLAYER

Four words: L-A-P-D
—explaining his decision not to move
west with the Dodgers

Rockwell, Norman
WHOLESOME AMERICANA ARTIST

Wanna hit?

—passing the pipe

Rollins, Ed

GOP POLITICAL CONSULTANT

I am deeply sorry for my stupid and insensitive remarks. In no way do they reflect the opinions of [candidate's name].

—form letter of resignation

Rommel, Erwin

NAZI FIELD MARSHAL

Fahrvergnügen.

—describing the pleasurable experience of driving a tank across North Africa

Rooney, Andy
HUMORIST

Did you ever notice that Jerry Seinfeld pretty much stole my act? I have.

Roosevelt, Franklin D.
THIRTY-SECOND U.S. PRESIDENT

Eleanor, it's one thing for me to see other women—but you?

——

It's not just fear itself. I am also petrified of cockroaches.
—therapy session

Rorschach, Hermann

PSYCHIATRIC PIONEER

Officer, that may look like a stop sign to you—but I see a cherry tomato playing a clarinet.

—trying to talk his way out
of a traffic ticket

Rubens, Peter Paul
PAINTER

Waiter! More pasta! More éclairs!
Eat up, girls! I'm painting
you in the morning!

Rushdie, Salman
AUTHOR/ISLAMIC HERETIC

Hi, this is Salman. I'm not in
right now. Please leave your
death threat after the beep.
—answering machine message

Ruth, George Herman "Babe"

BASEBALL LEGEND

Hey, ump! Take a look at that cupcake in the right field bleachers. She's got some set, huh?

—famous "called shot"

Sacco, Nicola

ANARCHIST

> *Let's blow up this Popsicle stand.*
>
> —remark to Vanzetti

Sam, Uncle

RECRUITER OF MEN

I WANT YOU

(If you want me, keep it to yourself.)

—clarifying "Don't Ask,
Don't Tell" policy

Sanders, Colonel

WAR HERO TURNED POULTRY KING

*"The Strategies and Recipes of
China's General Tso"*
—West Point term paper

Sandwich, John Montagu

ENGLISH EARL

*Absolutely delicious!
Note: placing roasted meats
between bread slices, rather
than vice versa, may reduce
messiness.*
—notes from food laboratory

*2 tbs. mayonnaise
2 tbs. ketchup
1 tsp. Indian relish*
—recipe for Secret Sauce

Schweitzer, Albert

HUMANITARIAN PHYSICIAN

I gave at the office.

Scowcroft, Brent

FORMER NATIONAL SECURITY ADVISER

Operation Man Tan
Operation Kurds and Way
Operation Second Term
Operation Wolf Blitzer
Operation Scowcroft
   —alternative suggestions for Gulf War
                     Operation Desert Storm

Scully, John

OUSTED CEO, APPLE COMPUTER

Fin@rly! A cunpter that c@n re@d ny h@mduuriting!!!

Seinfeld, Jerry

COMEDIAN

Some men see things as they are and ask "why?"

Shakespeare, William

ENGLISH PLAYWRIGHT

Fuck ye.

—nasty letter to theatre critic

Simmons, Richard

FITNESS FANATIC

> *If I couldn't exercise, I'd just go bonkers!*

Simpson, O. J.

SUSPECTED ATHLETE

> *And even after carving through this tin can, it's still sharp enough to slice a tomato!*
>
> *All in all, I'd rather be in Buffalo.*
> —*I Want to Tell You*, p. 8

Sinatra, Frank

CROONER

And now, your end is near.
And so you face your final curtain.
—last words to Sammy
"The Lungfish" Lillatello

Mark my words, boys: gangsta rap.
It's the next big thing.

Siskel, Gene

MOVIE CRITIC

No, Mom. It's me—Siskel.
Ebert's the fat one.

Sisyphus

FUTILITY PERSONIFIED

Zero bottles of beer on the wall.
Zero bottles of beer.
If one of those bottles should
happen to fall,
Zero bottles of beer on the wall.

A hundred bottles of beer on the wall,
A hundred bottles of beer . . .

—work song

Skinner, B. F.

BEHAVIORAL PSYCHOLOGIST

Kids, no dessert until you finish
your pellets.

kipper, the

STAWAY

I know I'm the one responsible for you being shipwrecked, Mrs. Howell. But there's got to be another way for me to make it up to you.
　　—the lost episode of *Gilligan's Island*

see also: Howell, Mrs. Thurston, III

Smith, Adam

FREE-MARKET ECONOMIC THEORIST

See this? I'm giving you the invisible finger.
　　　　—responding to criticism of his laissez-faire economic theory

Smith, Anna Nicole
MODEL

*You're a multibillionaire?
Honey, why didn't you tell me
that before we got married?*

Smith, Liz
GOSSIP COLUMNIST

*Afterward, my counselor **Marcy
Plotnick** made **Trudy Arnold,
Angela Romano,** and me clean
up the entire art shack. Then
Doris "D-Cup" Fenster
stopped in and just happened
to mention that she'd be going
to the **Boys Camp Cook-Out**
with **dreamboat Tommy
Feltham.***

—letter home from camp, age nine

Socrates

*Is this glass of hemlock half full
or half empty?*
>—last philosophical question

*Virtue is knowledge.
Ergo: Find dumb women.*
>—finding practical applications
>for his philosophy

Sorensen, Ted

JFK SPEECHWRITER

*What can you do for your country?
Don't ask.*
>—first draft

Spock, Mr.
STAR FLEET COMMAND

> Mr. *Spock? Mr. Spock is my father.*
> *Please, call me Dave.*

Stalin, Joseph
SOVIET DICTATOR

> *1. Complete toilet training*
> *2. Learn Russian*
> *3. Purge my family*
> —his first five-year plan

Steinbrenner, George
OWNER, NEW YORK YANKEES

> *How about a little credit for*
> hiring *so many managers?*

> *What do you mean, I can't?*
> —unsuccessful attempt to fire the
> manager of the St. Louis Cardinals

Stern, Howard
KING OF ALL MEDIA

> *I just want to be hated. Is that so wrong?*

Stevenson, Adlai
PRESIDENTIAL ELECTION SILVER MEDALIST

> *I am the egghead.*
> *Goo-goo-a-joob.*

Stewart, Martha
LIFESTYLE EXPERT

> *Disposable diapers are fine, but many mothers are going back to traditional cloth diapers.*
> —first words

Stone, Oliver

CONSPIRACY FILMMAKER

> *I'd like to thank the anti-Castro Cuban forces who made this award possible.*
> —Academy Award acceptance speech

Stone, Sharon

MOVIE STAR

> *Is there a window open? I feel a draft.*

Strasberg, Lee

ACTING COACH

> Be *the waiter.*

Streisand, Barbra
ENTERTAINER

"A Vision for Multilateral Diplomacy in a Meshugeneh World"
—address to UN General Assembly

Superman

MAN OF STEEL

> *I swear that's never happened to me before. . . . Are you sure your nightie isn't a kryptonite blend?*
>
> —embarrassing moment

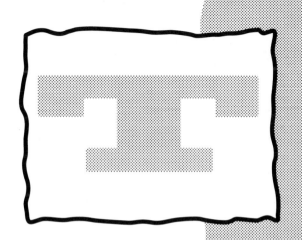

Tarzan

OF THE JUNGLE

I can't decide between Rainforest Crunch and Chunky Monkey.

Teresa, Mother

SAINT-ELECT

Kill the ref! Kill the ref!
—Notre Dame *vs.* USC, Rose Bowl 1992

Terrible, Ivan the

FIRST CZAR OF RUSSIA

*I can't decide whether to spell it
"czar" or "tsar."*
—first day on the job

Thomas, Clarence

SUPREME COURT JUSTICE

I can't define pornography, *but
I know it when I see it.*

I'll have whatever Scalia's having.
—decision on lunch

Thurmond, Strom
U.S. SENATOR

I don't dye my hair. I'm just prematurely orange.

Tiger, Tony the
SPOKESMAMMAL

They're prr-rrr-etty good!
—tasting early experimental prototype
of the frosted flake

Torquemada, Tomás de
SPANISH INQUISITOR

Funny, you look Jewish.

Treacher, Arthur
FAST-FOOD FISH MOGUL

Give a man a fish, feed him for a day.

Trebek, Alex
GAME SHOW HOST

I'm not a knowledgeable person but I play one on TV.

Trump, Donald
REAL ESTATE MOGUL

I don't care how many millions I make. I'll always cut my own hair.

Tse-tung, Mao

CHINESE COMMUNIST LEADER

I can't believe it. I'm already hungry for another revolution.

—twenty minutes after the first Chinese Communist revolution

Everybody have fun tonight. Everybody Tse-tung tonight.

—annual Communist Christmas party

—denied publishing demand

Unabomber

TERRORIST

This one absolutely, positively has to get there overnight!

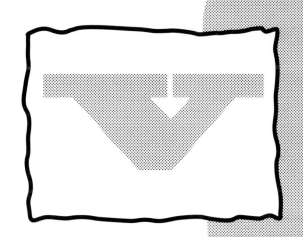

Valdez, Juan

COFFEE SPOKESMAN

> *Operator, I need a listing for the Maxwell Halfway House.*
> —coming to grips with his problem

Van Gogh, Vincent

ARTIST

*What the hell was I thinking?
How am I supposed to wear my
glasses?*

—afterthought

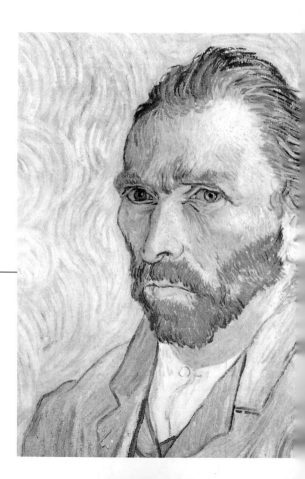

Vespucci, Amerigo
EXPLORER

The United States of Vespucci
Vespuccian Express
The Ugly Vespuccian
—contemplating possible namesakes

Vila, Bob
HOUSEHOLD EXPERT

Martha, nobody likes a
know-it-all.

Virgin Mary

MOTHER OF JESUS

*I don't care if my parents
believe me or not. It's the truth.*

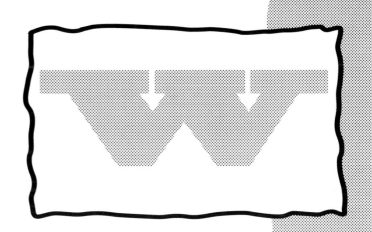

Waldheim, Kurt

AUSTRIAN POLITICIAN/UN SECRETARY GENERAL

Assistant Manager, The Gap,
Vienna, Austria, 1939–1944
　　　—suspicious résumé entry

Wallace, Mike

60 MINUTES INTERROGATOR

> *Shh! Listen. It's that damn ticking noise again!*

Walters, Barbara

TELEVISION JOURNALIST

> *Hello, we're live from Lillehammer, the lovely Olympic landscape, where the legendary luge event will lead off a little later.*
>
> —1994 Olympic coverage

Warhol, Andy
POP ARTIST

Soup is good art.

Warren, Earl
HEAD OF WARREN COMMISSION

After exiting the president's body, the bullet ricocheted around Dallas for two days until it entered the abdomen of Lee Harvey Oswald.
—first draft of the single-bullet theory

Washington, George

FIRST U.S. PRESIDENT

That doesn't look anything like me!

> —upon seeing the
> Washington Monument

Second *in war?*
Third *in peace?*
Fifth *in the hearts of my countrymen!?!?*

> —taking a dip in the polls

Westheimer, Dr. Ruth
SEX THERAPIST

*And our next caller, Ted from
Massachusetts . . .*

Will, George
TELEVISION CONTRARIAN

*If you keep quiet about my
clip-on bow tie, I won't tell
anyone about your clip-on hair.*
—secret pact with Sam Donaldson

Wilson, Woodrow
TWENTY-EIGHTH U.S. PRESIDENT

*Okay, then, how about this:
two leagues—the American and
National—and the winner from
each play in the World Series.*
—alternate proposal following rejection
of the League of Nations

Winfrey, Oprah

TALK-SHOW HOST

Lazy, pathetic, unemployable people who sit home and watch daytime television in a vain attempt to avoid confronting the cruel hopelessness of their failed lives.

—rejected show topic

Wright, Orville

FLIGHT PIONEER

In the event of a water landing, your seat cushion is a seat cushion.

—safety instructions to Wilbur

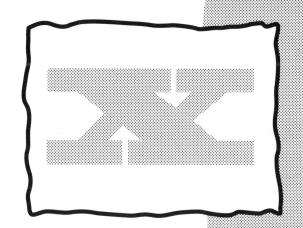

Xerxes

KING OF PERSIA

> *I defy you to name another character from history whose name begins with X.*
> —securing his place in the history books

X, Malcolm

BLACK NATIONALIST

How 'bout me, whitey?
—response to Xerxes

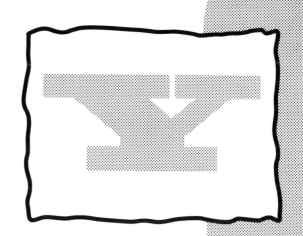

Yeltsin, Boris

RUSSIAN PRESIDENT

I know it's only 9 A.M.—but it's after noon in Siberia.

—sign on office desk

———

I think it's time to check back into the Raisa Gorbachev Clinic.

185

Zeus

GREEK GOD

Fellow gods:
In an effort to rule the universe
more efficiently, we will be
downsizing heaven and
terminating your positions. If I
can be of any assistance to you
in the future, please don't
hesitate to pray. (Ask for
"Yahweh.")
cc: Abraham

> —interoffice memo announcing
> monotheism

NOTE ON METHODOLOGY

The academic community will be pleased to learn that this ambitious work of revisionist history conforms to the established historical method. Once invented, each quote was scrupulously researched. For example: Countless hours were spent pouring through Napoleon's official archives and private papers (using primary sources whenever possible) to make certain he *never* said the words: *"Curse that Count de Custarde. I must invent a dessert of my own."*

That tedious process was applied to each entry herein. And when this work takes its place in the canon of Western literature, that effort will be repaid with the gratitude of contemporary academics and historians yet unborn.

TO / PICTURE CREDITS

Reach the author on the Disinformation Superhighway: notacorpse@aol.com